The Wood Design Awards 2002

A NORTH AMERICAN PROGRAM OF ARCHITECTURAL EXCELLENCE

Tuns Press
Faculty of Architecture and Planning
Dalhousie University
P.O. Box 1000
Halifax, Nova Scotia
Canada B3J 2X4
tunspress.dal.ca

Dean: Thomas Emodi
General Editor: Essy Baniassad
Managing Director: Donald Westin

The Wood Design Awards 2002

Editor: Don Griffith, Janam Publications Inc.
Design: Marie-Noëlle Massé, Janam Publications Inc.
Production: Donald Westin
Printing: Friesens

National Library of Canada Cataloguing in Publication

Wood Design Awards 2002 / edited by Don Griffith.

ISBN 0-929112-49-0

1. Building, Wooden – Canada.
2. Building, Wooden – United States.
3. Architecture – Awards – Canada.
4. Architecture – Awards – United States.
5. Architecture – Canada – 21st century.
6. Architecture – United States – 21st century.
I. Griffith, Don

NA4110.W66 2002   721'.0448'097109051   C2002-904533-9

Cover: Sisson Cottage, Bohlin Cywinski Jackson, M. Thomas Architectural Photography

The Wood Design Awards 2002

A NORTH AMERICAN PROGRAM OF ARCHITECTURAL EXCELLENCE

2002 SPONSORS

www.structurlam.com

DRICON
Fire Retardant Treated Wood

www.dricon.com

SUPPORTING
ASSOCIATIONS

www.aboutsfi.org

www.hardwoodcouncil.com

www.cwc.ca

The Wood Design Awards is the only North American Program to recognize and award excellence in wood architecture, and thus to acknowledge publicly the importance of architecture to our society.

The annual Program is open to new and remodeled residential and non-residential projects, and building interiors from the U.S. and Canada. Awarded projects push the conventional boundaries of wood as a construction and finishing material. Details on the Program and registration information may be found at www.WoodDesignAwards.com.

The Program is offered by Wood Design & Building and Wood Le Bois magazines [www.woodmags.com], and managed by Janam Publications Inc. We gratefully acknowledge the support of our sponsors and supporting associations: Structurlam Products Inc., Arch Wood Protection/Dricon, the Canadian Wood Council, The Hardwood Council and the Sustainable Forestry Initiative® [SFI], a program of the American Forest & Paper Association.

Don Griffith
Coordinator, *The Wood Design Awards*

The 2002 Jury

Brian MacKay-Lyons, Professor, NSAA, RAIC, RCA, (HON) FAIA, Brian MacKay-Lyons
Architecture and Urban Design, Halifax [left]

Brian MacKay-Lyons practices in Halifax, Nova Scotia where his firm focuses on houses, public buildings and urban design commissions. His renowned regionalist architectural language combines the use of archetypal forms with local building practices. His work has won local and international audiences, with publication in over 100 books and journals. His buildings have received some 53 awards including five Governor General's awards, four Canadian Architect awards, and three Wood Design awards. He is also a frequent lecturer.

Jeremiah Eck, FAIA, Partner, Jeremiah Eck Architects Inc., Boston [center]

Since establishing his firm in 1975, Jeremiah Eck has been guided by the principles that architecture is an art and a service, and that good clients make good architecture. His work is known for its attention to detail, craftsmanship, and sensitivity to the context of local architecture. His firm has won a number of national and regional awards, and two Wood Design awards, and has been published in over 150 books, journals and newspapers.

We thank our jurors for their devotion and care in selecting the 15 projects of the 2002 Program from a total of 320 submissions. Brief biographies of the jurors may be found at www.WoodDesignAwards.com.

Photo: Roy Grogan

Lawrence W. Speck, FAIA, Principal, PageSoutherlandPage, Austin [right]

Lawrence W. Speck has been described as one of eight "Emerging Voices" in American Architecture and as "one of 40 architects leading a new generation of American Architects" [Architectural League of New York]. His work has national recognition for its appropriateness to regional character. In the last ten years alone, he has won six national design awards, eight state awards, a Wood Design award, and 16 local awards. He recently served as the Dean of the School of Architecture, University of Texas at Austin.

Table of Contents

Toward a Culture of Wood Architecture

JIM TAGGART, MRAIC

Unique among building materials, wood has the capacity to humanize the structures and spaces we inhabit, and to articulate, through the art and craft of building, the intimate connection between culture and nature. In many northern countries this art has evolved over centuries to become an integral part of contemporary culture.

This is similarly evident in Japan, where years of aesthetic refinement and meticulous craftsmanship have combined to create an architecture that is at once elemental and elegant. With the Japanese reverence for wood that dates from antiquity, timber buildings have both shaped and reflected the culture for more than 1000 years. Today, wood is still valued for its unique visual and structural qualities and is given pride of place in many prestigious new buildings.

The role of timber in contemporary North American architecture is a less prominent one, although the roots of a timber culture do exist here. The continent's earliest timber structures were built by aboriginal people on the shores of the Pacific Northwest. Fashioned from cedar, these monumental post and beam longhouses with their towering totem poles were not only functional shelters but also powerful symbols of status, kinship and the veneration of ancestors.

Timber structures also occupied an important place in the psyche of the European cultures that settled North America from the 1600s on. Vast forests provided raw materials, first for the humble cottages, barns and boatsheds of the East Coast, then later for the factories, warehouses and mills that came to symbolize the strength and vigor of the emergent nations. These simple and robust structures defined the character of architecture on this continent until the early 20th Century.

But when the International Style of Modern Architecture caught hold in the 1950s, it brought a new palette of manufactured materials and a new sleek aesthetic for which the contemporary wood products seemed ill-suited. Only plywood and glue-laminated timber, with their modularity and dimensional stability, seemed suited to Modern buildings. Supported by a vast and lucrative housing market based on simple sawn lumber, the timber industry saw little benefit in modernization.

8

As a result, what emerged in North America were two distinct architectures: one for those buildings with wood structures, and a second for those built from other materials. The distinction was reinforced by prescriptive building codes that created separate classifications for combustible and non-combustible construction. Whereas new technologies such as prefabricated components and integrated building systems have been incorporated into other types of construction, wood structures have generally continued to be hand-built on site. While this vernacular approach undoubtedly produces many fine buildings, it has been unable to exploit the full potential of wood in the contemporary architectural context.

However, the situation is changing. With the growing desire to prevent further global warming, and conserve energy and resources, there has been a renewed focus on the management of our forests. Pressure to preserve our stands of old-growth timber is coupled with the realization that managed forests can provide a unique renewable resource for building, and make a positive contribution to the environment. A new value-added approach to forestry is emerging that will derive greater economic and environmental benefit from more efficient utilization of wood fiber.

The development of engineered wood products [EWPs], such as parallel strand lumber, laminated veneer lumber and wood I-joists, is only one aspect of a changing practice environment for architects and engineers. Building codes are moving to performance-based criteria for building design, promising new applications for wood. Computer numerically controlled [CNC] technology, used to cut and shape timber to tighter tolerances, will enable sophisticated, systematized approaches to structural design, and facilitating the improved integration of wood with other materials

These changes offer new possibilities to designers across North America, and have begun to bring a fresh new look to architecture in wood. The 15 projects selected in The Wood Design Awards, 2002 Program are testimony both to the continued vigor of our vernacular building tradition, and to the collective potential of advanced technology, composite construction and a more supportive code environment. Together, they represent the best of current practice and are a helpful step in establishing a culture of wood architecture in North America.

Honor Awards

Paint Rock Camp

CHARLES ROSE ARCHITECTS, INC.

Paint Rock Camp is part of a 110,000-acre cattle ranch located at the mouth of two small canyons at the south-western edge of the Big Horn Mountains in Wyoming. The Alm Foundation commissioned the architects to site and design a camp for 76 children from inner-city Los Angeles. The Alm Foundation program provides financial, counseling and academic support for promising underprivileged students throughout high school and college. Students spend their first three months in the program at Paint Rock Camp during the summer months.

The 16 buildings, that together provide 30,000sf of space, are divided into east and west sites and include cabins, a counselors' lodge, a directors' house, dining hall, kitchen, swimming pool and recreational areas. The buildings celebrate the natural landscape by being placed in specific response to the topography of the canyons.

At the east site location, the cabins are sited to the north where they hover above the canyon wall, and to the east, across a gully nestled into the land. They are lifted above the sloping ground on columns to minimize site disturbance and to exploit the remarkable views. The large dining hall, located at the center of the more populated east site, doubles as a great room.

The entire project was designed and built in 15 months. The remote location made trades and materials difficult to source thus increasing the challenge of the schedule. The material palette and construction method is indigenous to the surrounding environment. Materials consist of wood, steel, site-formed concrete and locally available river rock. Cabin framing is a combination of wood and steel, and 1x8 horizontal cedar siding. Large rolling screen doors and outer wood doors, suspended from hanging door tracks bolted to a steel header, open the cabins completely to the outdoors. The siding on the doors matches that of the cabin allowing the doors to blend easily with the overall structure when closed.

The dining hall is a heavy timber construction of reclaimed Douglas fir. Roof members are configured as inverted King post trusses with steel rods acting as tension chords. Each rod projects from the King post to either side of the dining hall where it connects to a clevis located at a beam-to-column inter-section. Wood dowels engage embedded steel plates that connect the wood members of the trusses. The dowels stand proud from the surface of the truss members for visual detail. The roof deck of tongue and groove 2x6 is supported on timber purlins that span across the trusses, and a section of the dining hall has a roof monitor to let in natural light. The roofs of all the buildings are finished with galvanized aluminum. Roofs are super insulated to eliminate the need for air conditioning in the cabins. Carefully sized windows, for example the awning windows adjacent to each bunk in the cabins, provide cross ventilation.

Jury

The low, jagged, angular forms of the buildings with their simple use of materials have energy and dynamism. The collection of roofs lifts off from the ground as if a topographic relief of the site.

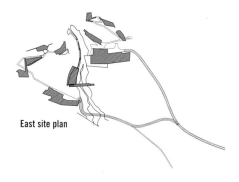

East site plan

14

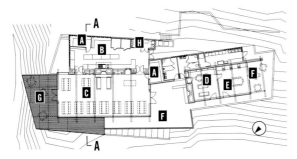

Dining hall plan

A	Storage	D	Library	G	Deck
B	Kitchen	E	Conference room	H	Mechanical
C	Dining	F	Terrace		

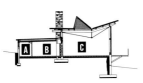

Section A-A

West elevation dining hall

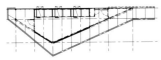

Plan

Plan

North elevation

East elevation

Section

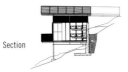

Section

Cabin 1

Cabin 3

Product Specs

FRAME
– Recycled Douglas fir timber frame in dining hall, steel and wood-frame in cabins, and wood platform frame in counselor and guest lodges; insulated plywood panel roofs finished with galvanized aluminum, tongue and groove 2x6 roof deck in dining hall

EXTERIOR
– Western red cedar drop siding and spaced boards, 1x8, and roof decks finished with clear stain

INTERIOR
– Concrete floors, painted drywall, maple millwork finished with clear stain

WINDOWS/DOORS
– Windows and doors of yellow cedar

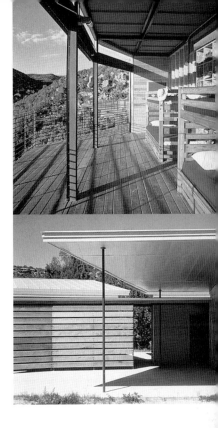

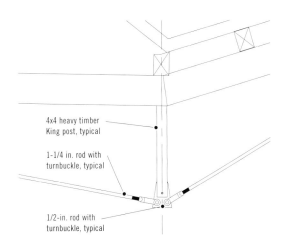

4x4 heavy timber
King post, typical

1-1/4 in. rod with
turnbuckle, typical

1/2-in. rod with
turnbuckle, typical

Inverted King post truss at dining room

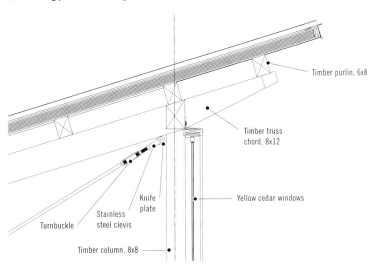

Timber purlin, 6x8

Timber truss
chord, 8x12

Knife
plate

Yellow cedar windows

Stainless
steel clevis

Turnbuckle

Timber column, 8x8

Inverted truss at dining room window

CLIENT
Alm Foundation
Woodland Hills, CA

ARCHITECT
Charles Rose Architects, Inc.
Somerville, MA

STRUCTURAL ENGINEER
Ove Arup & Partners
Cambridge, MA

GENERAL CONTRACTOR
Groathouse Construction, Inc.
Laramie, WY

PHOTOS
Chuck Choi Architectural Photography
Brooklyn, NY

Reeve Residence

CUTLER ANDERSON ARCHITECTS

A main program requirement of the clients was to keep their 2,800sf residence unobtrusive in a powerful waterfront landscape that borders the Strait of Juan de Fuca. The architects attempted to nestle the home into the cliff face by engaging in an exercise of camouflage.

The grass-covered roof is pitched at the "wind shear" angle of the nearby weathered trees to help it blend into the dominant shape of the land. The stone for the wall that borders the waterside terrace was selected and placed to fit into the rocky notch of the cliff where the building is located.

Living space is divided into three separate volumes: the bunkhouse, the great room with loft and the master suite. All are covered by a simple, bold shed roof that lowers the profile of the house from the water side. Passages between the living volumes allow easy movement between the water and forest sides of the house, thus establishing a strong connection to the landscape. The great room, facing south, fully opens up through sliding glass doors to the waterside terrace so the family can extend its living space into the sounds and smells of the Strait of Juan de Fuca.

The main support is a simple post and beam frame of separate roof eave and center beams and support columns for each of the three building volumes. A pleasing visual effect arises from the composite nature of the beams and columns that are, in fact, assemblies of four 2x lumber that sandwich steel flitch plates. Connections of a column at its base and beam support point are achieved using galvanized through bolts, covered with galvanized plugs. On the high side of the roof – the forest side – the composite columns are cross-braced with one lumber and one steel member for visual contrast. The beams and column assemblies take all vertical loads such that exterior walls act more like curtain walls and are generously inset from the roof perimeter.

The roof has two diaphragms: the lower full area diaphragm supported by an assembly of doubled 2x10 joists flanking a single 2x6 spaced at 16in. o.c., and an upper diaphragm of reduced area having a Derbigun waterproof membrane topped with a lightweight soil mix and native grasses. The roof joists supporting the upper diaphragm are 2x6 at 24in. o.c. A 4x6 pressure-treated timber "curb" borders the perimeter of both roof diaphragms. The lower diaphragm is built-up with 4in. of rigid insulation, an air space, plywood sheathing, and finally the waterproof membrane which extends over the curb where it is flashed and finished with a cedar fascia.

All joist ends on the north side are flush with the roof diaphragms and capped with protective galvanized steel that announces the roof construction as one approaches the house.

Jury

The home is a truly sustainable building because it starts with nature. It merges with the rock and flora of the landscape as if it grew there. The architecture is forceful and powerful, but still restrained.

Site plan
A Hot tub   D Great room
B Terrace   E Bunk house
C Master bedroom F Garage

Product Specs

FRAME
— Composite post and beam sections of
  wood with steel flitch plates; composite
  2x rafters and wood I-joist floor joists,
  wood stud interior partitions

EXTERIOR
— Western red cedar shingles, built-up
  Derbigum roof and partial metal roofing

INTERIOR
— Pine paneling on walls finished with
  semi-transparent solid stain, beech floors

WINDOWS
— Lindal Windows finished with latex stain

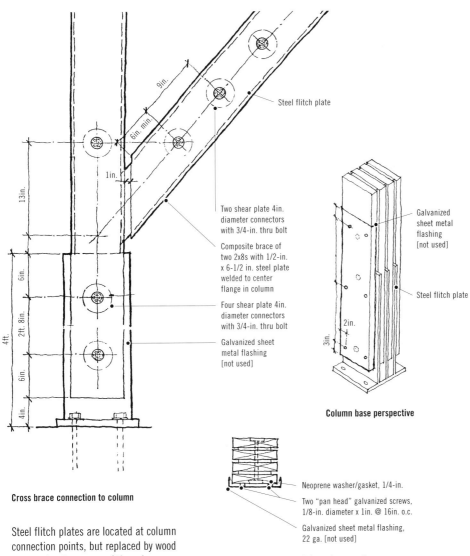

Steel flitch plate

9in.

6in. min.

1in.

13in.

6in.

2ft. 8in.

4ft.

6in.

4in.

Two shear plate 4in. diameter connectors with 3/4-in. thru bolt

Composite brace of two 2x8s with 1/2-in. x 6-1/2 in. steel plate welded to center flange in column

Four shear plate 4in. diameter connectors with 3/4-in. thru bolt

Galvanized sheet metal flashing [not used]

Cross brace connection to column

Steel flitch plates are located at column connection points, but replaced by wood spacers in other areas of the column.

Galvanized sheet metal flashing [not used]

Steel flitch plate

2in.

3in.

Column base perspective

Neoprene washer/gasket, 1/4-in.

Two "pan head" galvanized screws, 1/8-in. diameter x 1in. @ 16in. o.c.

Galvanized sheet metal flashing, 22 ga. [not used]

Column base section

CLIENT
The Reeves
Seattle, WA

ARCHITECT
Cutler Anderson Architects;
project architect: Janet Longenecker and
job captain: Julie Cripe, Bainbridge Island, WA

STRUCTURAL ENGINEER
Coffman Engineers, DeAnn Arnholtz PE
Spokane, WA

GENERAL CONTRACTOR
Russet Construction, Spud Grimes; Brett
Ackerman, carpentry; Dan Nichols, cabinetry;
Tony Rodhiger, stone mason, Lopez, WA

PHOTOS
Art Grice Photographer
Bainbridge Island, WA

Agosta House

PATKAU ARCHITECTS INC.

A private residence of 2,775sf was built for a couple relocating from Manhattan to San Juan Island, a small, largely rural island off the Pacific coast in Washington State. In addition to the usual domestic requirements, the program included an office, in which the couple intend to continue their professional work, and a garden enclosed by a12ft. high fence for protection from roaming deer.

The site consists of 43 acres largely covered by second-growth Douglas fir forest, 10 acres of which have been dedicated to a perpetual conservation easement. The actual site of the house within the larger property is a grassed meadow, enclosed on three sides by the dark fir forest, but open to the northwest where it overlooks rolling fields below and, beyond across Haro Strait, to the gulf islands of British Columbia.

The house is stretched across the ridge of the meadow, almost as a spatial dam, to divide the meadow into an enclosed forecourt to the southeast, a sort of spatial reservoir that is released through the house to the panorama below of picturesque fields and waterways.

The building section is "battered" in which walls and roof slope in response to the gentle slope of the site. The organization of the house is the result of pushing out and manipulating its simple section by creating exterior recesses that subdivide the house programmatically into general planning zones, and by inserting non-structural bulkheads that organize the interior into finer spatial areas.

Product Specs

FRAME
– Wood stud walls, exposed Douglas fir
  beams, rafters, purlins and decking;
  concrete slab on grade

EXTERIOR
– Standing seam steel, western red cedar
  channel siding; Cabot stains

INTERIOR
– Vertical grain Douglas fir veneered
  plywood finished with teak oil; exposed
  concrete floors

WINDOWS/DOORS
– Custom made using Douglas fir

The concrete slab-on-grade house is conventionally framed with exposed Douglas fir rafters on 2ft. centers, and 2x4 and 2x6 wall studs on 16in. centers finished with painted gypsum board. Radiant heating is achieved with hot water distributed in tubing cast into the slab.

Most of the walls consist of standard construction of air barrier, sheathing, batt insulation and poly-ethylene. However, in cases where the roof line bends down to form the wall, a 3-1/2 in. layer of rigid insulation was added over the interior faces of 2x4 studs to achieve continuity of the moisture barrier between the roof and wall. The roof similarly uses rigid insulation but has pressure-treated wood strapping let-in on 2ft. centers to attach the roofing.

The exterior is prominently clad in light-gauge galvanized sheet-steel which is intended not only to protect the structure from the normal effects of weather, but also addresses the possibility of wildfire in an area not well served by firefighting services. Western red cedar siding also makes up the cladding on some walls stained to color-match the steel cladding.

Jury

The house is remarkable for its abstractness yet is so completely rooted to its site. It takes its lead completely from the slope of the site and emulates nature in the architectural style of Alvar Aalto.

Section A-A at living room/kitchen looking south-west

Section B-B at entry looking southwest

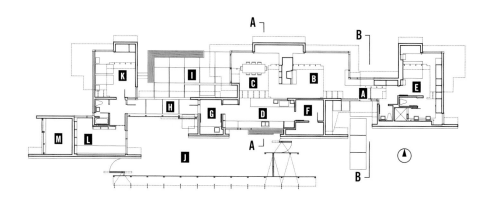

Floor plan

A	Entry	F	Storage / mechanical	K	Guest room
B	Living room	G	Mud room	L	Studio
C	Dining room	H	Covered walkway	M	Garden shed
D	Kitchen	I	Terrace		
E	Master bedroom	J	Fenced garden		

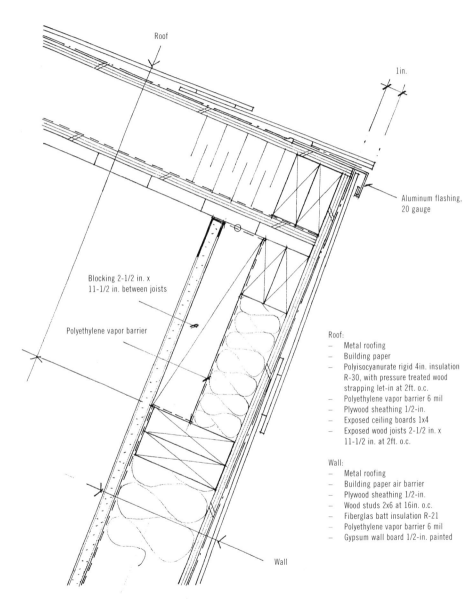

Roof

1in.

Aluminum flashing,
20 gauge

Blocking 2-1/2 in. x
11-1/2 in. between joists

Polyethylene vapor barrier

Roof:
- Metal roofing
- Building paper
- Polyisocyanurate rigid 4in. insulation
  R-30, with pressure treated wood
  strapping let-in at 2ft. o.c.
- Polyethylene vapor barrier 6 mil
- Plywood sheathing 1/2-in.
- Exposed ceiling boards 1x4
- Exposed wood joists 2-1/2 in. x
  11-1/2 in. at 2ft. o.c.

Wall:
- Metal roofing
- Building paper air barrier
- Plywood sheathing 1/2-in.
- Wood studs 2x6 at 16in. o.c.
- Fiberglas batt insulation R-21
- Polyethylene vapor barrier 6 mil
- Gypsum wall board 1/2-in. painted

Wall

Roof/sloping wall section

CLIENT
The Agostas
San Juan Island, WA

ARCHITECT
Patkau Architects Inc.
John Patkau, Patricia Patkau, David Shone

STRUCTURAL ENGINEER
Fast + Epp
Vancouver, BC

GENERAL CONTRACTOR
Ravenhill Construction
San Juan Island, WA

PHOTOS
James Dow
Edmonton, AB

Merit Awards

Jackson-Triggs Niagara Estate Winery

KUWABARA PAYNE MCKENNA BLUMBERG ARCHITECTS

Nestled in the Niagara wine region of southern Ontario, the Jackson-Triggs Niagara Estate Winery represents the effort of the vintner to complement the success of its wine label with a significant architectural presence on a 26-acre estate vineyard site.

The building's simple form unites production and hospitality functions under a single continuous roof plane that is supported along the length of the building by 60ft. clear-span inverted glued-laminated Douglas fir trusses with doubled parallel glulam top chords, all held in tension by boldly detailed steel brackets and tie rods that emanate from a steel node. The trusses extend through the clerestory glazing to support the roof overhang. Contrasted with the unfinished galvanized metal roof deck, the wood trusses, with their combed finish, recall the Ontario agrarian tradition of "post and beam" farm buildings, and eliminate the need for rows of columns and numerous load-bearing interior walls.

The Great Hall, a large two-story court with 20ft. high motorized glass doors at either end, serves to orient the visitor to the winery's amenities – tours, tasting bar, café, retail shop and administrative offices – and creates a convertible space that opens to the breezes and surrounding vineyards in mild weather. A screen of Douglas fir slats sets off the steel stair and, in combination with white oak wall panels, window and door frames, brings warmth to the interior palette.

The industrial character of the production areas is contrasted with the more refined design of the public and guest services areas. Custom millwork in the tasting rooms, café, and V.I.P. lounge, crafted of white oak indigenous to the region, refers to the French and American oak casks found in the barrel and storage cellars. Oak is used extensively for flooring throughout the V.I.P. lounge and dining areas.

The winery exemplifies the values of contemporary sustainable architecture, setting an environmentally sensitive precedent for a number of future wineries currently being developed in the grape-growing regions of Canada.

Merit Award

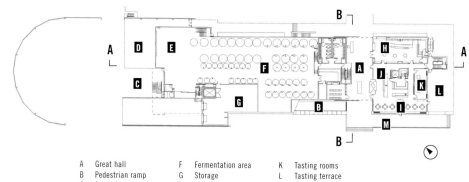

A	Great hall	F	Fermentation area	K	Tasting rooms
B	Pedestrian ramp	G	Storage	L	Tasting terrace
C	Service court	H	Retail shop	M	Café terrace
D	Crushing area	I	Café		
E	Pressing area	J	Wine bar		

Ground floor plan

Jury

The strength of the project lies in its systemic use of numerous types of details. It has extraordinary and pleasing clarity of detail and assembly of pieces that will be understood by all who use and visit the building.

Section A-A

Section B-B

Product Specs

FRAME
– Glulam Douglas fir trusses, purlins and beams [combed finish] and tensile steel rod connections by Goodfellow, Delson, QC; steel frame walls

EXTERIOR
– Cement board siding, steel deck roof and membrane roofing, mezzanine guards and service court fence of clear western red cedar planks finished with exterior wood sealer

INTERIOR
– Walls of quarter cut white oak veneer, ceilings of quarter cut Douglas fir veneer panels, Douglas fir slat siding doors finished with clear catalytic lacquer, oak floors in VIP lounge and dining areas

WINDOWS/DOORS
– Aluminum frame by Fulton Windows, Mississauga, ON

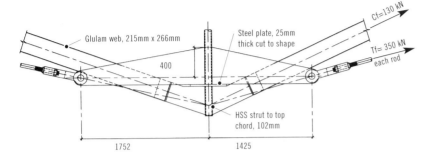

Cf=130 kN

Tf= 350 kN
each rod

Glulam web, 215mm x 266mm

Steel plate, 25mm
thick cut to shape

400

HSS strut to top
chord, 102mm

1752   1425

Elevation of Douglas fir truss at steel node [courtesy Blackwell Engineering Ltd.]

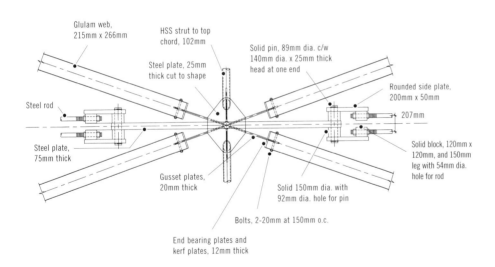

Glulam web,
215mm x 266mm

HSS strut to top
chord, 102mm

Steel plate, 25mm
thick cut to shape

Steel rod

Solid pin, 89mm dia. c/w
140mm dia. x 25mm thick
head at one end

Rounded side plate,
200mm x 50mm

207mm

Steel plate,
75mm thick

Gusset plates,
20mm thick

Solid 150mm dia. with
92mm dia. hole for pin

Solid block, 120mm x
120mm, and 150mm
leg with 54mm dia.
hole for rod

Bolts, 2-20mm at 150mm o.c.

End bearing plates and
kerf plates, 12mm thick

Plan of Douglas fir truss at steel node [courtesy Blackwell Engineering Ltd.]

The inverted glulam trusses span 60ft. and bear on steel columns located in the long walls. For optimal structural efficiency, the glulam elements are stressed in compression and steel tie rods in tension. However, the 4in. diameter steel rods that extend from the steel node to each of the paired glulam top chords transfer compression loads from the top chords to the node, much in the manner of the center post in a King post truss.

CLIENT
Vincor International Inc.
Mississauga, ON

ARCHITECT
Kuwabara Payne McKenna Blumberg
Architects
Toronto, ON

STRUCTURAL ENGINEER
Blackwell Engineering Ltd.
Toronto, ON

CONSTRUCTION MANAGER
Merit Contractors of Niagara
St. Catherines, ON

LANDSCAPE ARCHITECT
Janet Rosenberg & Associates Inc.
Toronto, ON

PHOTOS
Peter A. Sellar/KLIK
Oakville, ON [p. 40 and 43]
and Design Archive/Robert Burley
Toronto, ON [p. 38, 39, 41 and 42]

Kansas Plains Wedding Chapel and Pavilion

ROCKHILL AND ASSOCIATES

On an open field of brome grass adjacent to the childhood home of the bride was constructed a temporary pavilion and chapel. The vaulting sky, pervasive light and arcing horizon of the Kansas landscape are evident in its design.

After the vows were recited the reception took place back under the pavilion, a Lamella arch construction spanning a 1-1/2 in. thick concrete floor poured directly onto the field and reinforced with a fiber additive. The slab has since been cut into 3ft. x 3ft. squares for use in patios, driveways and sidewalks.

The Lamella arch is a graceful and simple way to create large spans with common materials. Essentially, it is a curved roof framed by a system of interlocking arches. The arches have beveled ends that are bolted together. Once it is in place and the horizontal thrust at the sidewalls is counteracted, the roof acts as a skin in which every member supports the others and shares the load.

The Lamella arch was constructed with 2x10s each just less than 10ft. long. Using a worm drive saw and a jig the upper edge of each member was cut to the same arc as the overall structure. The individual lamellas were secured with salvaged 7in. stainless steel bolts and nuts resulting in the visually dramatic diamond pattern.

The 40ft. x 75ft. rectangular Lamella-arch roof rested on reused laminated veneer lumber beams that span a series of recycled utility poles set into holes dug into the field. The poles were stabilized with manila ropes that created diagonal bracing above the arch and were tied to pipe stakes driven into the ground. At each utility pole a cable spanned to the corresponding column on the opposite side. The cables helped to keep the columns from splaying and also supported caged work lights that illuminated the space.

Merit Award

After the first morning's dew evaporated the canvas roof covering shrank to a drum tight translucent shelter. The sidewalls were constructed with salvaged 4x4 redwood mounted to the utility poles with simple steel "forks" that were easily adjusted allowing us to create a gentle curve. Horizontal slats of used flooring gathered these posts and supported the simple burlap that defined the space.

The chapel represented the complex order of the natural flora, with its rich symmetry that blooms from the ground and delivers the unexpected. It was built with felled cottonwood trunks enclosed with a tight weave of limbs and saplings screwed to the trunks. The altar was a slab of stone leftover from a masonry project and the planters to each side were concrete bathtub experiments from the past.

Maple paths of salvaged gym flooring connected chapel, pavilion and house. The pavilion has been dismantled and stored for future use.

Jury

Here is an exquisite use of wood in its natural form that responds beautifully to the prairie landscape where objects stand stark and solitary. There is a poetic quality to these temporary wood structures that should be more often seen in permanent buildings.

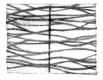

Chapel

Product Specs

CHAPEL
– Cottonwood trunks and branches

PAVILION
– Recycled utility poles, LVL [laminated veneer lumber beams], 2x10 Lamella construction connected with 7in. stainless steel bolts and covered with canvas, 2x4 purlins, 4x4 redwood posts, recycled Douglas fir flooring and burlap for walls

PATHS
– Maple flooring recycled from a gymnasium

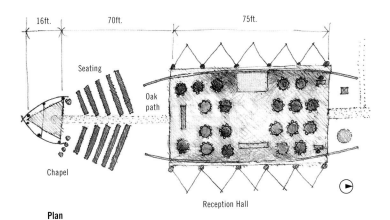

16ft.   70ft.   75ft.

Seating

Oak
path

Chapel

Reception Hall

Plan

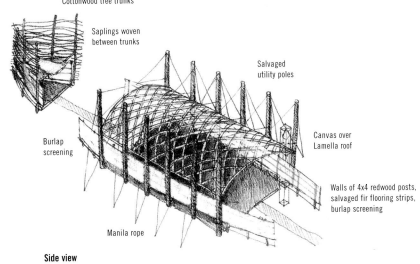

Cottonwood tree trunks

Saplings woven
between trunks

Salvaged
utility poles

Burlap
screening

Canvas over
Lamella roof

Walls of 4x4 redwood posts,
salvaged fir flooring strips,
burlap screening

Manila rope

Side view

CLIENT
Hannah Rockhill and Ian Hurst, bride and
groom
Lecompton, KS

ARCHITECT
Rockhill and Associates,
Dan Rockhill and David Sain
Lecompton, KS

GENERAL CONTRACTOR
Rockhill and Associates

PHOTOS
Dan Rockhill

View Silo House

ROTO ARCHITECTS, INC.

The 1500sf house sits on an ancient bank of the now receded Yellowstone River, the only sheltering feature in a valley of the Absoroka Mountains famous for wind, grand views and large storms. After investigating several approaches, client and architect chose not to mimic the horizontal character of the valley floor. They also wished to avoid the status quo massing and blocky proportions that typify other dwellings in the valley, and which often lack any connection to earth and sky. The architects chose the region's grain silos and elevators as a model, adapting their vertical organization and minimal, but dramatic, skyprint.

The View Silo occupies the smallest practical footprint and the narrowest possible sliver of sky. The house tapers and appears to twist. Entry is at grade with bedrooms below the crest of the bank, and partially embedded in the earth. As the silo narrows toward the third level, a mezzanine for cooking and eating is located within the tapering double height volume. Above this point, the stair tower becomes open to the sky and terminates in a rooftop observatory. Its slatted perimeter provides a filtered 360-degree view but tends to force the eye skyward.

The platform frame construction uses a combination of 2x6 studs, I-joists and lumber joists supported at mid-span by bearing walls. The roof is a 2 in 12 pitch surmounted by the observatory. The south and east walls are clad by a layered system of 2x2 vertical cedar slats, selected for their relationship to traditional agricultural out buildings in the valley. The slats are face screwed to 2x strapping over a waterproofing of brick-red asphalt roll roofing. The slats thus lift from the surface of the roll roofing by a 1-3/4 in. gap to dematerialize the façade. Slat spacing varies from 1/2-in. to 2-1/2 in. to differentiate areas of the elevations. The larger spacing shows a hint of the red roofing when the sun is direct, while the narrow spacing always reads as a shadow.

Product Specs

FRAME
– Wood frame mainly 2x6, CDX plywood and oriented strand board 3/4-in., masonry block

EXTERIOR
– Wall: CDX plywood, Tyvek, Ice Buster 2, rolled asphalt roofing, cedar 2x2 slats and 1x8 boards. Roof: Tongue and groove plywood, Ice Buster 2, corrugated galvalume

INTERIOR
– Western hemlock and vertical grain Douglas fir casings around interior windows and doors, clear water-based sealer finish

WINDOWS/DOORS
– Windows and Exterior doors by Pozzi

Ground floor plan

Second floor plan

A Bedroom
B Balcony
C Bathroom
D Entrance
E Storage
F Walkway
G Living
H Office
I River room
J Porch
K Kitchen

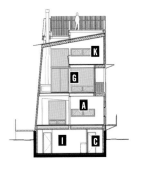

Section A-A

Section B-B

West elevation

North elevation

Jury

The house has a strong sculptural form that fits the rugged landscape. The vertical slats make a "delaminating" or "subtracting" skin in contrast to the solidity of the mountains.

Mounting brackets 1-1/2 in. x 3in. x 1/4-in. steel angle 2in. long at 32in. o.c.; attach after installation of roll-on roofing

Continuous steel angle 1-1/2 in. x 1-1/2 in. x 1/4-in. at 32in. o.c. pre-assembled to 2x2 slats with 3/8-in. x 1in. steel bolt welded thru angle

Pre-finished metal flashing 1/8-in. thick installed under roll-on roofing at header and over at sill

1in.

Slats 2x2

Roll-on roofing

Air barrier

Vapor barrier

1-3/4 in.

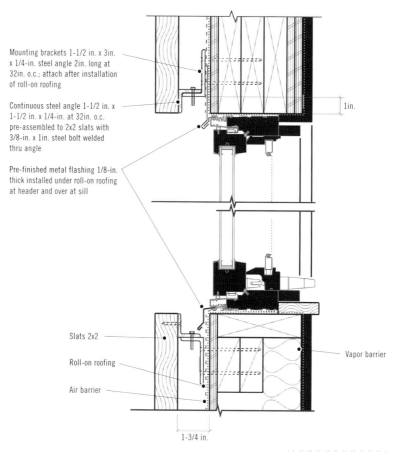

Typical window detail

The original mounting detail with steel clips and angles, as shown in the drawing, allowed the slat façade to be panelized with no visible sign of fasteners. The architect changed the detail to face fastening with screws on 2x strapping to save material and labor costs.

Mounting of 2x2 slats

Vertical 2x2 slats at 1/2-in. or 2-1/2 in. spacings

CLIENT
Ron Gompertz
San Francisco, CA and Livingston, MT

ARCHITECT
RoTo Architects, Inc.,
Clark Stevens, AIA, APA Principal
Los Angeles, CA and Livingston, MT

STRUCTURAL ENGINEER
MT Structural, John Schlegelmilch, Principal
Bozeman, MT

GENERAL CONTRACTOR
Ron Gompertz
San Francisco, CA and Livingston, MT

PHOTOS
©2001 Larry Stanley, Stanley Photography
Livingston, MT [p. 50, 51, 52, 54 and 55]
and RoTo Architects, Inc. [p. 53]

River Tower and Studio

ANDERSON, MASON, DALE ARCHITECTS

This family retreat incorporates a variety of small wood buildings. The tower at 12ft. square and 50ft. high makes a high perch of seclusion for meditation and reading as an adjunct to the adjacent 12ft. x 36ft. studio. The tower captures views of the surrounding 14,000ft. peaks, the Arkansas river and redtail hawks that nest in nearby rock cliffs. The studio is a drawing room for two architects. Both buildings were built by architecture students from the University of Cincinnati. They prefabricated some parts of both buildings in the university shop and were involved in on-site construction.

The new buildings are placed in proximity to a main cabin and guest cabin in a manner that recalls a village composition of the early gold mining settlements of the area. The tower and studio are companion elements that celebrate the joy of study and work as an undivided experience. A stair that winds around the open center shaft of the tower leads to a platform under the room that surmounts the tower. A ladder and hatch give access to the room which is fitted with built-in seating and storage for overnight sleeping closer to the stars. The studio includes a raised work area at each end of its nave-like space, a metaphor to step up to one's work with total focus and devotion.

The tower is a steel frame clad with spaced 2x6 southern pine boards screwed to 2x6 studs that are bolted to saddles welded to the steel frame. The spaced siding allows the tower to glow as a lantern in the night sky. The room on top is a simple 2x6 wood frame and steel construction supporting a flat, sloped roof of 2x6 joists and plywood sheathing topped with a single-ply membrane. Four composite beams of nail-laminated 2x6 lumber transfer roof loads to the walls. The simple gable roof of the studio is framed with batt-insulated 2x6 rafters that span to a ridge beam. Spruce 1x6 shiplap siding finishes the interior walls and ceiling.

Jury

The project represents an elemental and iconic use of western imagery. The gable roof of the studio and the box lantern of the tower are strongly rendered complementary elements.

57

Site plan

Product Specs

FRAME

– Tower: steel frame surmounted by room of 2x6 glass wall construction and partial steel framing supporting composite nail-laminated 2x6 roof beams and a flat, sloped roof assembly of 1x6 ceiling boards, 2x6 joists, and single-ply membrane on plywood. Studio: wall studs and rafters 2x6, and floor joists, 2x12

EXTERIOR

– Southern pine boards 2x6; studio deck of redwood 2x6 finished in pigmented clear stain; tower roof finished with elastomeric sheet and studio with metal roofing. Studio windows: Marvin Windows

INTERIOR

– Shiplap spruce 1x6 on studio walls and ceiling, floor slate and maple, built-ins with Baltic birch plywood; custom poplar doors and wood windows in both tower and studio

LUMBER AND MILLWORK

– Reed Mill & Lumber Co., Inc., Denver, CO

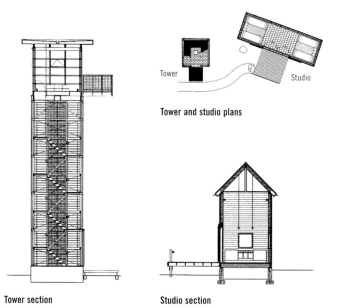

Tower and studio plans

Tower section

Studio section

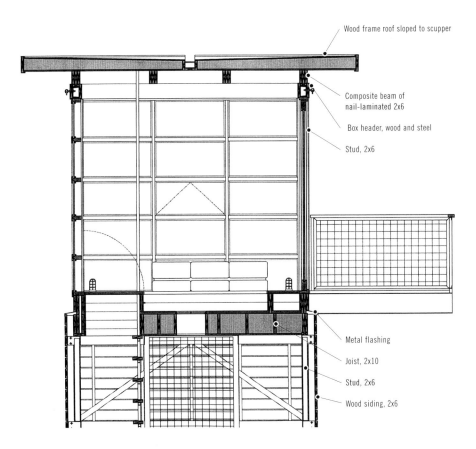

Wood frame roof sloped to scupper

Composite beam of
nail-laminated 2x6

Box header, wood and steel

Stud, 2x6

Metal flashing

Joist, 2x10

Stud, 2x6

Wood siding, 2x6

Tower room

CLIENT
Ron Mason, FAIA
Denver, CO

ARCHITECT
Anderson, Mason, Dale Architects,
Ron Mason, FAIA; Kiel Moe, project architect
Denver, CO

STRUCTURAL ENGINEER
Martin/Martin Inc., Chuck Keyes
Wheat Ridge, CO

PHOTOS
Greg Hursley, Austin, TX
[p. 56 to 59 and 61 top] and Frank Ooms,
Denver, CO [p. 60 and 61 bottom]

Albrecht Residence

SALMELA ARCHITECT

The site of the 5,742sf house sits 80ft. above the main channel of the Mississippi River traffic on Lake Pepin. It borders a dense pine forest on the east and is very close to a neighboring house to the west. The clients, a local newspaper publishing couple, like to entertain and wanted the home to capture the warmth of wood common to a Minnesota cabin but having the formality of Architecture.

The L-shaped plan uses both traditional gable and flat roofs that sets up a contrast in house forms. A long gable running along the west property line creates a private court open to the south face of the house and the forest to the east. A formal procession from the street moves past the stand-alone garden house/garage and passes below a Douglas fir and cedar pergola at the main entrance. Bedrooms are separated from the main living space. The main living and entertaining area opens to the garden court on the lake side of the site, and to the second story library and screened porch. A painted wood slat screen borders the stair and separates the kitchen from the living area.

Recycled material is used structurally as well as for finishing surfaces. Reclaimed Douglas fir timbers, redwood from old wine vats, cypress from vinegar vats, and new wood brought the total number of wood species used to seven.

The construction is essentially lumber platform framing that incorporates heavy timber beams and columns. The scale of reclaimed timbers was maintained and used to their maximum span for honesty of structure. Only the massive Douglas fir columns are over designed in their application. They stand almost as art objects and no one had the heart to scale down the magnificent old timbers.

Despite the use of natural materials and traditionally gabled roofs that act as bookends on the east and west, the house commands a refined, modern feel that makes the traditional elements seem shocking.

Site plan

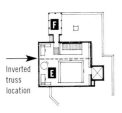

Inverted truss location

Second floor

A   Entry
B   Living/dining
C   Kitchen
D   Court
E   Office/library
F   Screen porch
G   Master suite
H   Laundry
I   Bedroom
J   Garage
K   Garden house

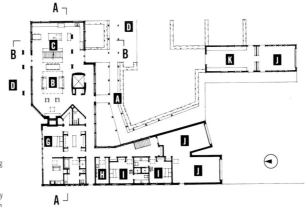

A

D

B

B

D

A

A

Ground floor

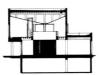

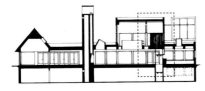

Section A-A looking north   **Section B-B looking east**

Jury

The project stands out for its rich use of wood species that is skillful and not overwhelming, and for its varied set of building forms. The house has a beautiful northern quality, a Scandinavian quality.

Product Specs

FRAME
— Wood framing, reclaimed heavy timber

EXTERIOR
— Recycled cypress siding and trim, western red cedar soffits, brick veneer, slate, granite block; galvalume standing metal seam roof and Duralast membrane

INTERIOR
— Douglas fir, recycled redwood, pine and basswood paneling, Douglas fir ceiling boards, cherry floors amd gypsum board; recycled Douglas fir and maple casework

WINDOWS/DOORS
— Douglas fir aluminum clad, Douglas fir doors

FINISHES
— Clear exterior stain, one coat; natural oil and paint on interior wood

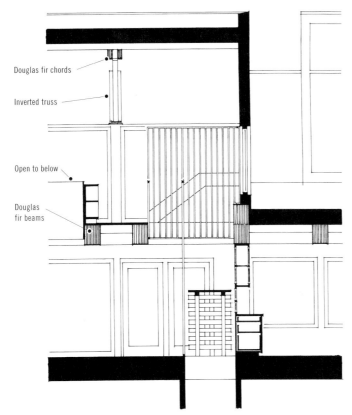

Douglas fir chords

Inverted truss

Open to below

Douglas fir beams

Detail, section A-A
[See corresponding photo left]

Position of truss

The inverted truss in the library is used as a device to reduce visually the ceiling height, an essential ingredient in the comfort of the room. Its asymmetrical quality, in which the greatest depth is not at mid-span, is so the lowest point centers on the floor opening. Thus, when viewed from below, it looks logical.

CLIENT
The Albrechts
Redwing, MN

ARCHITECT
Salmela Architect
Duluth, MN

STRUCTURAL ENGINEER
Carroll, Franck & Associates
St. Paul, MN

GENERAL CONTRACTOR
Alms Construction and River City Builders
Redwing, MN and Nerstrand, MN

LANDSCAPE ARCHITECT
Coen + Stumpf + Associates
Minneapolis, MN

COLORIST
Carol Stumpf Design
Minneapolis, MN

PHOTOS
Peter Bastinelli Kerze
Eveleth, MN

Citation Awards

Gosline Residence

BOHLIN CYWINSKI JACKSON

The owners were open minded about architecture that pays heed to the nature of materials and the expression of the way things are put together. The result is an interior that is both lively and calm, playful and contemplative, that makes strong visual use of basic building materials.

The open layout of the 2,100sf house includes a second floor master bedroom that overlooks the living room, two offices that can double as guestrooms, and refinements such as a mail-sorting nook shielded by a small sliding barn door.

Exposed structure begins at the approach walkway that borders a street-level carport framed in cedar and translucent polycarbonate panels. Visible wood beams, joists and rafters trace regular patterns over the narrow width of the house. A central spine of steel columns and C channel beams extend through the entire length of the house and project out of the three-story rear wall.

Structure is also expressed in millwork and finish carpentry. The stair beyond the entrance foyer, for example, uses maple stair treads that weave through and are supported on horizontal maple boards placed on edge. The open risers filter light and offer views to the interior, both vertically and horizontally.

Positioned to preserve two important site trees, the home is a narrow 20ft.-wide platform frame construction of 2x6 studs, 24in. o.c. sheathed with 1/2-in. plywood sheathing and clad with fiber cement panels.

Floors are simply framed with 2x10 joists in exposed areas, and with 9-1/2 in. wood I-joists in enclosed areas. Beams, 4x10 on 8ft. centers, span from one exterior wall to the central steel spine and on to the opposite exterior wall. Rafters span between the beams.

Spaces between rafters were filled with foil-faced batt insulation and finished with recessed plywood fastened to 2x2 strips. The top of the insulation is fitted with a baffle leaving a 1-1/2 in. air space followed by 1/2-in. plywood roof sheathing, bituminous paper and standing seam metal roofing.

Jury

The project has a clear, dynamic plan on a difficult, narrow lot, and a construction that is full of promise.

71

Product Specs

FRAME

- 2x6 stud Douglas fir walls, steel columns and C channel beams; 2x12 rafters [select structural where exposed], 2x10 floor joists, 9-1/2 in. TJI/PRO I-joists and 4x10 beams. Plywood CDX sheathing, 1/2-in.

EXTERIOR

- Fiber-cement panels with solid color stain, galvanized steel horizontal flashings, polycarbonate glazing.
- Standing seam painted steel roof over plywood sheathing.
- Douglas fir stile and rail doors, custom Bobinga wood front door. Ipé wood on outdoor decks.

INTERIOR

- Horizontal maple slats, stair treads and cabinetry, maple Apple-Ply wall panels, polycarbonate glazing, tongue and groove Douglas fir decking on upper floor. Integrally colored concrete floor at lower floors.

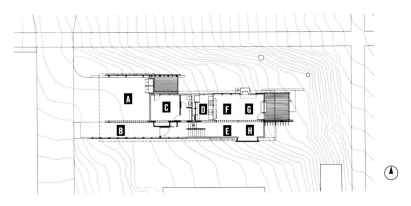

First floor plan

A   Carport
B   Main approach walkway
C   Office/guest room
D   Kitchen
E   Main hall
F   Dining
G   Living
H   Sitting room

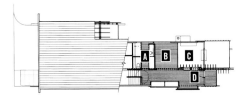

Second floor plan

A   Main bath
B   Main bedroom
C   Open to below
D   Reading room

Basement floor plan

A   Crawl space with access
B   Office

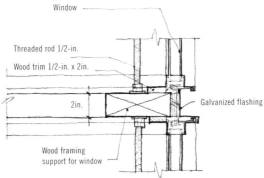

Window

Threaded rod 1/2-in.

Wood trim 1/2-in. x 2in.

2in.

Galvanized flashing

Wood framing
support for window

Section at mid-points

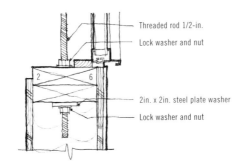

Threaded rod 1/2-in.

Lock washer and nut

2   6

2in. x 2in. steel plate washer

Lock washer and nut

Section at base

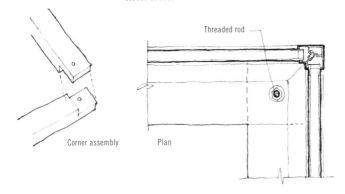

Threaded rod

Corner assembly   Plan

**Plan and section details of threaded rod through wood framing
support at floor-to-ceiling corner window**

CLIENT
The Goslines
Seattle, WA

ARCHITECT
Bohlin Cywinski Jackson
Wilkes-Barre, PA, Pittsburgh, PA,
Philadelphia, PA, Seattle, WA, Berkeley, CA

STRUCTURAL ENGINEER
Putnam Collins Scott Associates
Seattle, WA

GENERAL CONTRACTOR
Eric Thorsen Construction, Inc.
Seattle, WA

PHOTOS
James Frederick Housel [p. 73 top and 75],
Karl Backus [p. 72, 73 bottom] and Benjamin
Benschneider [p.70, 71 and 74]

Beaverton City Library

THOMAS HACKER AND ASSOCIATES ARCHITECTS INC.

Today's public library is no longer viewed as only a repository of books, but more as an information center and community meeting area. Following this idea, the new Beaverton City Library has become one of the busiest libraries of its size in the U.S. and is a key element in the development of a new urban center for the City of Beaverton.

With 69,000sf, the library houses a 150-seat auditorium, public meeting rooms, reading rooms, a personal computer room, and Youth Services and Young Adult Services areas. The library also includes space for an extensive audio-visual and electronic media collection.

The design makes use of light-filled open spaces for reading and browsing. It follows a simple, well-articulated form and an understated dignified theme that emphasizes the natural beauty of materials and crafted construction. Site design by the landscape architects has created a welcoming place for numerous city events.

Pre-cast concrete and masonry bearing walls support pre-cast concrete floor units. The large center portion of the roof rests on 26ft.-tall tree-like structures of glued-laminated timber [glulam].

Glulam achieved the necessary structural properties while representing a solid member appearance. Each of the 64 branches is made from 3/4-in. laminations of Douglas fir, about half the thickness of regular laminate pieces, to allow for a sharper bending radius. The design of the columns reinforces the City of Beaverton's slogan, "The City of Trees."

The goal was to create a roof of strongly expressed structure that was also light and floating. Thus, the columns support a main lattice of 5-1/8 in. x 12in. glulam purlins on 14ft. centers. Two similar but lighter lattice systems are installed above the main lattice, and topped with 2x6 tongue and groove decking applied in a parquet-like pattern. Above the decking lies a single-ply roofing of non-ventilated rigid insulation board and membrane.

Product Specs

ROOF FRAMING
– Wood deck panels supported on three "lattice" systems of diagonal solid and glulam purlins, main purlins: 5-1/8 in. x 12in.; glulam columns at 28ft. o.c. with splayed branches supporting main purlins 14ft. o.c.

GLULAM SPECIFICATIONS
– 24F-V4 DF glulam columns, individual laminations of 3/4-in., by Stimson Lumber

EXTERIOR
– Single ply, rigid board in walls and roof, masonry and precast exterior walls

INTERIOR
– Alder panels and millwork, satin varnish finish

Site plan

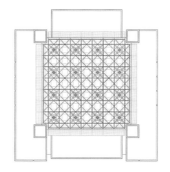

Reflective ceiling plan

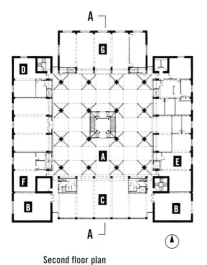

A

G

D

A

F   E

B   C   B

A

Second floor plan

Section A-A

A   Reading Room
B   Meeting Room
C   Periodicals
D   Juvenile Services
E   Work Room
F   Staff Lounge
G   Business Information

Jury

The library succeeds on many fronts: rigorous geometry, clear synchronization of structural elements, craftsmanship in detailing, and interaction of light and space. The delicate and unassuming roof contrasts well with its muscular support structure.

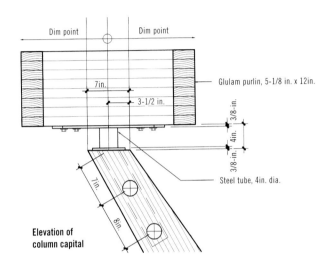

Dim point   Dim point

7in.

3-1/2 in.

Glulam purlin, 5-1/8 in. x 12in.

3/8-in.
4in.
3/8-in.

7in.

8in.

Steel tube, 4in. dia.

**Elevation of
column capital**

CLIENT
City of Beaverton, OR

ARCHITECT
Thomas Hacker and Associates Architects Inc.
Portland, OR

STRUCTURAL ENGINEER
kpff Consulting Engineers
Portland, OR

CONSTRUCTION
Drake Construction
Portland, OR

LANDSCAPE ARCHITECT
Walker Macy
Portland, OR

PHOTOS
Dave Davidson [p. 79 and 80], John Hughel
[p. 76 and 81] and Stephen Miller [p. 77 and 78]
Portland, OR

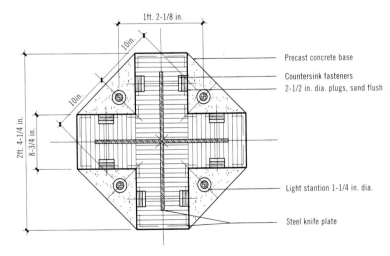

1ft. 2-1/8 in.

10in.

10in.

2ft. 4-1/4 in.

8-3/4 in.

Precast concrete base

Countersink fasteners

2-1/2 in. dia. plugs, sand flush

Light stantion 1-1/4 in. dia.

Steel knife plate

Plan of column base

Nicola Valley Institute of Technology

BUSBY + ASSOCIATES ARCHITECTS LTD. AND EQUILIBRIUM CONSULTING INC.

The first building of the 48,532sf Nicola Valley Institute of Technology campus, a shared native and non-native institute, reflects both the culture of aboriginal students and provides a modern education facility of classrooms, faculty offices, social spaces, labs, bookstore, cafeteria and library. Using native building forms of historic pit houses, the 400ft.-long crescent-shaped building tucks into a north hillside for minimal site disturbance. The lower section of the roof is planted with indigenous plants that moderate heating and cooling loads. Site preservation included tree conservation and storm water retention among the parking areas.

The building defines the beginning of a circular court with a ceremonial arbor oriented on the cardinal points, with the main entrance on the east axis to symbolize the start of day. A central fireplace greets students inside the main east entrance and provides preheating for the glazed ventilation atrium. The project performs 35% below ASHRAE standards for energy efficiency by employing thermal mass, an efficient envelope, natural ventilation, and solar control.

The structure is highly innovative in its combination of wood and concrete. Wood, most efficient in compression and part of the local architectural heritage, was used mainly as columns. The 256 main floor and second floor columns, respectively 300mm and 250mm in diameter, are facetted glulam produced by Structurlam Products Ltd. using a CNC [computer numerically controlled] cutting machine. Supporting loads as high as 50 tons, the columns connect to the slabs with cast ductile steel elements. The glulam columns were installed after the slabs by inserting them in place of the shoring towers, an operation that took only 20 minutes per column.

The central atrium is fully glazed above the roofline and framed with glulam columns that cantilever past the roof slab to carry lateral loads. Wood frame construction completes the atrium roof. The choice of wood stud curtain walls instead of steel was based on sustainable design commitment, support for local industry, and compatibility with the yellow cedar envelope.

82

Jury

The project has a very sincere environmental agenda through its profile, placement on the site, choice of materials to minimize embodied energy, and energy efficiency. The light European-style cedar skin is appropriate and binds the building to the site.

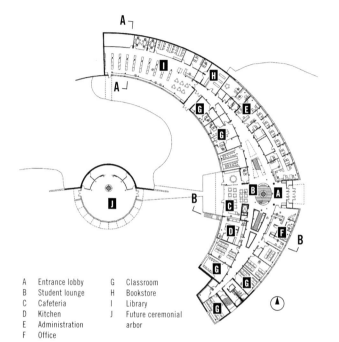

A	Entrance lobby	G	Classroom
B	Student lounge	H	Bookstore
C	Cafeteria	I	Library
D	Kitchen	J	Future ceremonial
E	Administration		arbor
F	Office		

Main floor

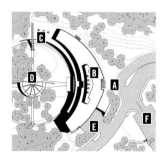

A	Entry plaza
B	Ventilation atrium
C	Planted roof
D	Future ceremonial arbor
E	Loading dock
F	Parking

Site plan

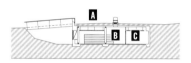

Section A-A

A	Planted roof	E	Classroom
B	Library	F	Lab
C	Seminar	G	Ventilation atrium
D	Office	H	Internal street

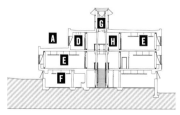

Section B-B

Product Specs

FRAME
— Wood-frame roof and glulam frame of beams and facetted columns in place of more typical steel framing used with concrete slabs, 265mm thick, 30-50% recycled fly ash content. Glulam by Structurlam Products Ltd., Penticton, BC

EXTERIOR
— Alaskan yellow cedar in rainscreen envelope system, and in sunscreens over windows, unfinished; wood stud curtain walls

INTERIOR
— Acoustic ceilings in library and main entrance 1x6 cedar slats, alder wood floor at central fireplace, maple doors, countertops and handrails; concrete slabs and shearwalls left exposed

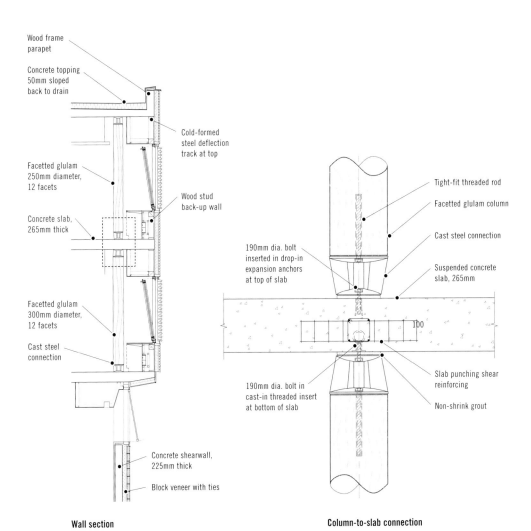

Wood frame parapet

Concrete topping 50mm sloped back to drain

Cold-formed steel deflection track at top

Facetted glulam 250mm diameter, 12 facets

Wood stud back-up wall

Concrete slab, 265mm thick

Facetted glulam 300mm diameter, 12 facets

Cast steel connection

Concrete shearwall, 225mm thick

Block veneer with ties

Wall section

Tight-fit threaded rod

Facetted glulam column

Cast steel connection

Suspended concrete slab, 265mm

190mm dia. bolt inserted in drop-in expansion anchors at top of slab

100

Slab punching shear reinforcing

190mm dia. bolt in cast-in threaded insert at bottom of slab

Non-shrink grout

Column-to-slab connection

CLIENT
Nicola Valley Institute of Technology and
The University College of the Cariboo
Merritt, BC

ARCHITECT
Busby + Associates Architects Ltd.
Vancouver, BC

STRUCTURAL ENGINEER
Equilibrium Consulting Inc.
Vancouver, BC

GENERAL CONTRACTOR
Swagger Construction
Abbotsford, BC

LANDSCAPE ARCHITECT
True [TR Underwood] Engineering
Kelowna, BC

PHOTOS
Nic Lehoux Photography
Vancouver, BC

Sisson Cottage

BOHLIN CYWINSKI JACKSON

The 70-acre ocean front Goosewing Farm is almost completely surrounded by water. The farmland gently rises 50ft. above sea level to a cluster of original 17th and 18th century cottages and agrarian structures.

The owners purchased the property with the intent of creating a distinctive, multigenerational family compound. The 5,400sf Sisson Cottage, an 18th century residence renovated and enlarged, is the first stage in this undertaking.

From the gabled roof and modest exterior, clad with traditional cedar shingle and shake, rise two chimney-like metal clad monitors. One of the monitors contains a wood sheathed light well around which wraps a stair that connects all floors. Natural light filters down the center of the stair through a Douglas fir screen of structure and lath that recalls the lath and plaster finish of the original walls. A nearly imperceptible, removable panel at the second floor provides access to a ladder leading to rooftop views of the ocean and countryside. Interior wood shutters along the stair provide views to the home's interior.

The first floor living area was opened up to create a modernist plan punctuated with Douglas fir columns and beams in place of bearing walls. Newly installed antique heart pine flooring subtly discloses the locations of former wall partitions. A boulder fireplace animates the interior.

Much of the original framing was left intact, with standard platform framing used for the new load-bearing and partition construction. The addition carefully matches floor and rooflines through the use of laminated veneer lumber framing. In addition to the lath screen walls of the light well, interior wall finishes vary from painted plaster veneer to "floating" vertical grain Douglas fir boards furred out from the plaster walls to create a reveal between plaster and wood.

A theme of revealing wood lath, framing and tongue-and-groove boards occurs throughout the cottage. The idea of expressing "how things go together" was used in the detailing of casework to unify the overall renovation and new construction.

Citation Award

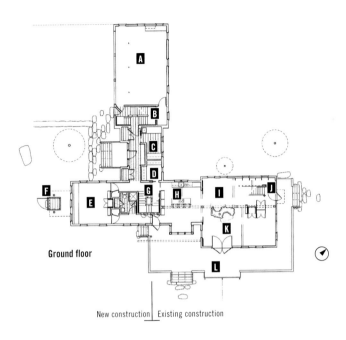

Ground floor

New construction | Existing construction

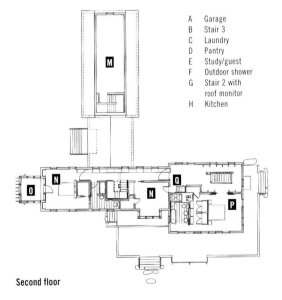

Second floor

A   Garage
B   Stair 3
C   Laundry
D   Pantry
E   Study/guest
F   Outdoor shower
G   Stair 2 with
     roof monitor
H   Kitchen

I   Dining
J   Stair 1
K   Living
L   Deck
M   Loft/storage
N   Bedroom
O   Sleeping porch
P   Master bedroom
Q   Stair to attic bedroom

Jury

*The renovation and new construction
is skillfully handled so that it is difficult
to tell where the old house stops and
the new begins. The mix of old and
new details recall the magic of the
original historic house.*

91

Product Specs

FRAME
– Platform wood framing with Douglas fir
 columns and beams by The G.R. Plume
 Company, Ferndale, WA; laminated veneer
 lumber framing in new roof and floor

EXTERIOR
– Eastern white cedar shingles with semi-
 transparent "Driftwood Gray" stain by
 Cabot; western red cedar roof shingles

INTERIOR
– Douglas fir lath screens, painted plaster
 veneer, vertical grain Douglas fir boards
 installed horizontally, furred-out paneled
 walls, antique heart pine floors; low-luster
 polyurethane and paint finishes

WINDOWS/DOORS
– Custom made with Spanish cedar by
 Manning Design, Fall River, MA, custom
 interior doors of vertical grain Douglas fir

MILLWORK
– Vertical grain Douglas Fir lumber and
 plywood with low luster polyurethane
 finish

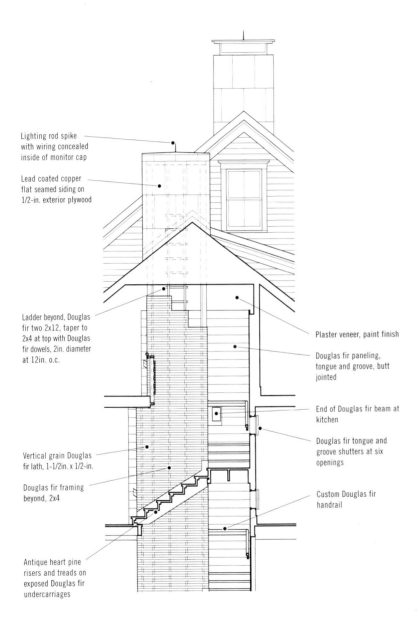

Lighting rod spike with wiring concealed inside of monitor cap

Lead coated copper flat seamed siding on 1/2-in. exterior plywood

Ladder beyond, Douglas fir two 2x12, taper to 2x4 at top with Douglas fir dowels, 2in. diameter at 12in. o.c.

Vertical grain Douglas fir lath, 1-1/2in. x 1/2-in.

Douglas fir framing beyond, 2x4

Antique heart pine risers and treads on exposed Douglas fir undercarriages

Plaster veneer, paint finish

Douglas fir paneling, tongue and groove, butt jointed

End of Douglas fir beam at kitchen

Douglas fir tongue and groove shutters at six openings

Custom Douglas fir handrail

Section at stair 2 showing roof monitor and light well in elevation
[All Douglas fir vertical grain]

ARCHITECT
Bohlin Cywinski Jackson
Wilkes-Barre, PA, Pittsburgh, PA,
Philadelphia, PA, Seattle, WA, Berkeley, CA

STRUCTURAL ENGINEER
Ryan-Biggs Associates, P.C.
Troy, NY

GENERAL CONTRACTOR
Charles E. Millard, Inc.
Bristol, RI

LANDSCAPE ARCHITECT
Michael Vergason Landscape Architect
Arlington, VA

PHOTOS
M. Thomas Architectural Photography
Exeter, PA

The Jones Farmstead

SALMELA ARCHITECT

The farmstead is located in the rolling farmland of southern Minnesota. The owners are restoring their 137 acres to native grassland and stressed the importance of having their new home fit the farming heritage of the township.

In addition to the main 6,500sf house, there is a guest house and barn that together employ a mix of construction materials: wood framing, heavy timber, poured concrete, bricks and logs. The two-story U-shaped plan of traditional gable roofs encloses a garden that has a centrepiece of formally spaced trees. Large windows admit natural light that illuminates the interior wood finishes. The finishes, which include maple flooring, Douglas fir paneling and heavy timbers, maple casework, painted basswood and pine logs, literally coat most surfaces but are used with skill to communicate refinement rather than rusticity.

All structures of the farmstead are primarily built with wood that in some cases performs a dual role as both structure and finish. Simple wood trusses are used in the garage for its 107ft. length. The guest space is built as a traditional log structure that completes the diversity of construction styles yet is not disruptive of the total statement.

The house combines platform wood framing and rafters with heavy timber. The main wing of the house has a central spine consisting of a timber truss with webs that punch through the second floor loft to connect with the top chord that forms the roof ridge. The top chords project from the gable roof ends of the west elevation to anchor large roof overhangs framed with 2x10 lumber.

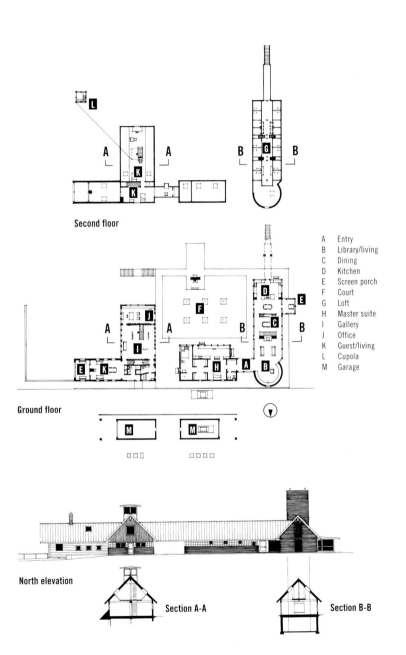

Second floor

A	Entry
B	Library/living
C	Dining
D	Kitchen
E	Screen porch
F	Court
G	Loft
H	Master suite
I	Gallery
J	Office
K	Guest/living
L	Cupola
M	Garage

Ground floor

North elevation

Section A-A

Section B-B

Jury

The skill of this project must be appreciated because its directness in conforming to a vernacular architectural style approaches the sublime.

97

Product Specs

FRAME
– Wood framing, heavy timber, poured concrete, bricks and logs

EXTERIOR
– Recycled cypress siding and trim, western red cedar soffits, brick veneer, slate over stucco, log; stained, oiled or left natural

INTERIOR
– Maple flooring, Douglas fir paneling and heavy timbers, maple casework, painted basswood, Douglas fir millwork; stained, oiled or varnished

WINDOWS/DOORS
– Douglas fir aluminum clad, Douglas fir doors

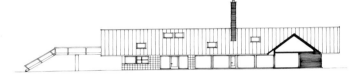

West elevation

Central roof truss, west elevation

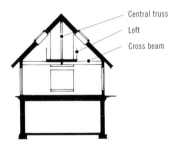

Central truss
Loft
Cross beam

Section west living area

The top chord projects from the gable roof ends of the west elevation
to anchor large roof overhangs framed with 2x10 lumber.

ARCHITECT
Salmela Architect
Duluth, MN

STRUCTURAL ENGINEER
Carroll, Franck & Associates
St. Paul, MN

GENERAL CONTRACTOR
River City Builders
Nerstrand, MN

LANDSCAPE ARCHITECT
Coen + Stumpf + Associates
Minneapolis, MN

COLORIST
Carol Stumpf Design
Minneapolis, MN

PHOTOS
Peter Bastinelli Kerze
Eveleth, MN

The Avis Granary

FERNAU & HARTMAN ARCHITECTS, INC.

The 1,200sf granary is part of a ranch compound that includes a renovated ranch house and a new car barn and workshop. The granary had been abandoned and forgotten for 50 years and suffered considerable damage. The architects treated the granary as a "found object." Thus, they approached its renovation to a bunkhouse and multi-purpose gym and theatre as an act of discovery, recovery and reappropriation of the ranch compound.

The program was ambitious given the building's cellular organization and exoskeletal structure. What was there and what was given weighed heavily in favor of the status quo. The architects faced the question of how strongly to intervene. Their answer was to re-purpose rather than preserve. The granary was seen as the foil, not the container, for their intervention. To that end, they proceeded both backwards and forwards in architectural time, seeking to re-establish the integrity of the original wood-frame and clad structure while re-purposing it for housing people and leisure activity.

A new architectural language was required that would not hide the intervention of the renovations. What is old is obviously old, and what is new is visibly new. The added insertions include a retractable steel stair, new fenestration, wood frame sleeping towers built into the interior corners and clad with stained horizontal Douglas fir siding, and a projecting window clad in standing-seam metal.

The greatest challenge was not the accommodation of the new program but the resolution of a multitude of small details where old met new. This required a careful interweaving on site of new and salvaged wood products. For example, new glulam beams span 20ft. from the new interior sleeping towers to the opposite wall still clad with the original pine boards, and large medium density fiberboard panels are placed vertically along a portion of the original interior walls.

Product Specs

FRAME
– Wood framing

EXTERIOR
– Douglas fir siding, stained, western red cedar roof shingles and copper roofing

INTERIOR
– Recycled Douglas fir, medium density fiberboard, and maple flooring, all finished with clear sealer; new Douglas fir paneling stained; maple casework

WINDOWS/DOORS
– Wood, painted

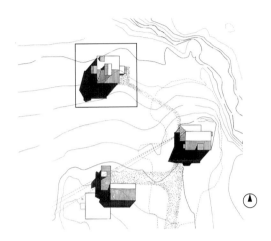

Site plan
Granary [top], shed, house [right]

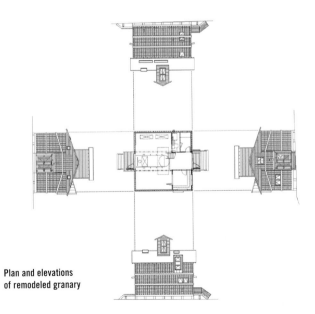

**Plan and elevations
of remodeled granary**

Jury

*The joy of this project is that it brings a
new purpose without losing the qualities
that make it a traditional building. It
provides modern, functional living space
without being pretentious or fussy.*

103

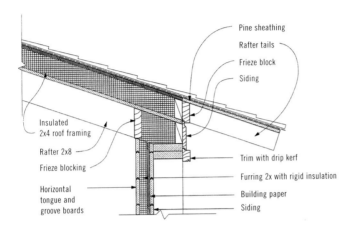

Pine sheathing
Rafter tails
Frieze block
Siding

Insulated
2x4 roof framing

Rafter 2x8

Frieze blocking

Horizontal
tongue and
groove boards

Trim with drip kerf

Furring 2x with rigid insulation

Building paper

Siding

Granary roof eave

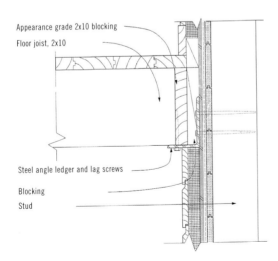

Appearance grade 2x10 blocking

Floor joist, 2x10

Steel angle ledger and lag screws

Blocking

Stud

Framing of second story stair landing of granary to main wall

CLIENT
The Avis'
Palo Alto, CA

ARCHITECT
Fernau & Hartman Architects, Inc.
Berkeley, CA

STRUCTURAL ENGINEER
Bridger Engineers, Ed Matos
Bozeman, MT

GENERAL CONTRACTOR
Anzick Construction
Livingston, MT

LANDSCAPE ARCHITECT
Sandy Blake
Big Timber, MT

PHOTOS
J.K. Lawrence/jklawrencephoto.com
Bozeman, MT

Gilmore Skytrain Station

BUSBY + ASSOCIATES ARCHITECTS LTD. AND FAST + EPP

The Gilmore Skytrain Station in the city of Burnaby, adjacent to Vancouver, occupies a low visibility location next to the site of a future high-rise building. Site and budget constraints called for a simple, economical, yet architecturally unique expression. The solution has a strong engineering quality arrived at by the close association of the architects and structural engineers.

The Gilmore Station is one of several for a new extension of the public light rail transit system. The design theme for all was to use wood to create a distinctive West Coast ambiance. Wood has histori-cally been dismissed as an inappropriate material for transit stations. However, design parameters were established so that that wood elements remained out-of-reach of vandals, have no direct weather exposure, and have a minimum 45-minute fire-resistance rating.

The project makes a feature of the various elevators, stairs and escalators to celebrate the movement of people as they come and go. A transparent effect was important, thus essential elements include open, clear spaces, the use of glass for visibility, and generous canopies for protection from wind and rain. The wood component consists of 64 identical timberstrand board panels, each 2.4m wide x 5m long, supported by simple structural steel frames spaced at 5m. The fabricator pre-bowed each 38mm-thick panel using weights, the resulting curve being maintained through the use of 10mm diameter stainless steel wires and custom-cast iron support arms and fittings. The panel and steel units were then inverted and covered with a roofing membrane that sheds water into gutters incorporated into the steel channel beams and round columns. From inside the station, transit users experience the visual warmth of the exposed wood panels.

The roof structure took only two days to erect and represents a novel application of an economical engi-neered wood product. The curved canopy roof lends a "high-tech" look that can be seen from a distance. The walls and roof were designed in a modular fashion for reconfiguration and adaptation to future development around the site.

106

Jury

The transit station shows a highly imaginative use of a wood shell in an urban setting. The roof vault represents an incredible marriage of structure and shelter.

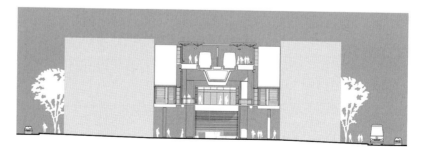

Elevation

108

Timberstrand board panel set on supports

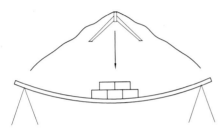

Weights added to bow panel, steel support placed with slack cables

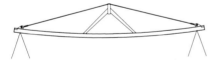

Weights removed and cables tightened

Roof panel units inverted and installed on beam and column supports

Roof panel fabrication

Product Specs

FRAME

— Precast concrete and steel structure, with 64 timberstrand board panels 38mm thick, 2.4m wide x 5m long supported by steel frames on 5m centers; roofing membrane and glass curtain walls. Roof structure by StructureCraft Builders Inc., Vancouver, BC

CLIENT
Rapid Transit Project 2000
Burnaby, BC

ARCHITECT
Busby + Associates Architects Ltd.
Vancouver, BC

STRUCTURAL ENGINEER
Fast + Epp
Vancouver, BC

GENERAL CONTRACTOR
Dominion Construction
Vancouver, BC

LANDSCAPE ARCHITECT
Durante Kreuk Ltd.
Vancouver, BC

PHOTOS
Nic Lehoux Photography
[p. 107, 108, 109 bottom, 110 and 111]
and Gerhard Welsch [p. 106 top and 109 top]
Vancouver, BC

110

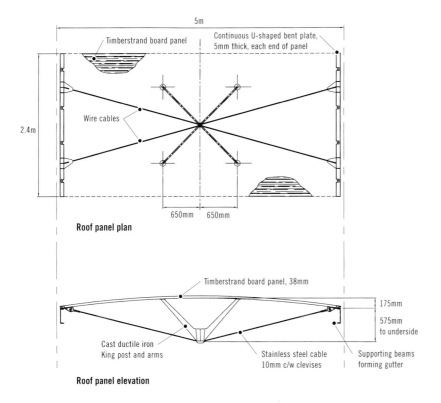

5m

Timberstrand board panel

Continuous U-shaped bent plate,
5mm thick, each end of panel

2.4m

Wire cables

650mm   650mm

Roof panel plan

Timberstrand board panel, 38mm

175mm

575mm
to underside

Cast ductile iron
King post and arms

Stainless steel cable
10mm c/w clevises

Supporting beams
forming gutter

Roof panel elevation

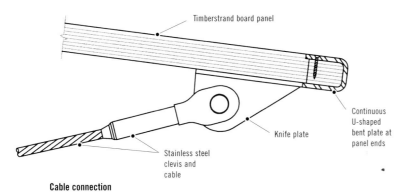

Timberstrand board panel

Continuous
U-shaped
bent plate at
panel ends

Knife plate

Stainless steel
clevis and
cable

Cable connection

111

OTHER PUBLICATIONS BY TUNS PRESS

Architecture Canada 2002 : The Governor General's Medals for Architecture
ISBN 0-929112-48-2, 2002

Barry Johns Architects : Selected Projects 1984-1998
ISBN 0-929112-32-6, 2000

Architecture Canada 1999 : The Governor General's Medals for Architecture
ISBN 0-929112-45-8, 2000

Brian MacKay-Lyons : Selected Projects 1986-1997
ISBN 0-929112-39-3, 1998

Works : The Architecture of A.J. Diamond, Donald Schmitt & Company, 1968-1995
ISBN 0-929112-31-8, 1996

Patkau Architects : Selected Projects 1983-1993
ISBN 0-929112-28-8, 1994

A Pictorial History of St. Paul's Anglican Church, Halifax, Nova Scotia
ISBN 0-929112-19-9, 1993

For additional information, please see our website at tunspress.dal.ca

The Wood Design Awards complete information and registration at: www.WoodDesignAwards.com